# GORDON PARKS

## *A Poet and His Camera*

# GORDON PARKS :

*Preface: Stephen Spender*

# A Poet and His Camera

BY GORDON PARKS

*Introduction: Philip B. Kunhardt, Jr.*

A STUDIO BOOK · THE VIKING PRESS · NEW YORK

WI

*For Elizabeth and Leslie*

# PREFACE

Mr. Gordon Parks is one of the most remarkable living photographers. The pictures in this book are of animals, children, beautiful women, men engaged in various kinds of action, towns, and nature. That he is a poet with his camera as well as with his pen, shows, I think, in his concentration on the image. His photographs nearly always leave a single, strong, clear image in the mind, or else contrasted images. The dove against the wall; the figures of the jockeys—at once brilliantly colored and yet ghostly—coming up against the long white line of a fence; the marvelous image of the speedboat in which the wake of the boat seems to be transforming the quiet weave of the waters in the foreground into straight white parallel horizontal lines. All these are true, and even poignant.

In presenting the image Mr. Parks has great concentration. When we see a photograph of a girl holding a fan, we think first of the fan, then of the eyes, which are seen and seeing through it, then of the calmly holding hand.

With images so poetic in themselves, one is curious whether the poems can add anything to them. They succeed, I think, because Mr. Parks does not strain to make them do so. One reads a poem for itself and then, as one turns to the photograph—which may obviously, or less obviously, be related—something seems added to the poem, and something also to the photograph.

In a few cases there is a more direct relationship between poems and photographs. This is true of the photographs of children which, with their simplicity, are among those I like best. "To Alain" begins:

> There's me!
> Shining in the water-sun!
> There's me!
> With all the fishes, weeds and things! . . .

And sure enough in the photograph nothing could be more Alain with all the fishes, weeds and things.

The charming portrait opposite the poem "Kansas Land" of a boy lying in the grass is also very closely connected with the richly pleasing, closely packed description of the farmlands in a poem which ends with the sweet yet angry lines:

> . . . All this I would miss—along with the fear, hatred
> and violence
> We blacks had suffered upon this beautiful land.

The poems can be read for themselves, and the photographs looked at for themselves. But if you look at the pictures and read the poems, without knowing quite why, they enrich one another and add up to a larger sum of enjoyment.

STEPHEN SPENDER

# ON GORDON PARKS

Two springs ago Gordon Parks and I worked on a photographic story together. It was to be the story of Everyman, told by a sequence of pictures starting with birth and babyhood, the child, and adolescence, and stretching to marriage, parenthood, struggle, satisfaction, the nobility of old age.

This remarkable photographer—a long-time associate of mine at *Life* magazine but first and foremost a dear friend—came to my house in the country to take one of the pictures he was after. He wanted to show the marvelous exuberance, the wilderness of a child, and he had chosen my eight-year-old daughter as his subject. He found his spot in a wooded meadow. In a late-afternoon orange light he set up his camera with a very long lens amidst a tangle of weeds, mustard plants, and dripping goldenrod, so that yellow and green sprays swayed out of focus across his lens. This would give the real subject of the picture—far back in the woods—a magical, unreal cast. Squatting in the weeds, his eye fixed to the camera, he directed my daughter in the distance as she bounced out of the woods with her red dog crashing at her heels, breakneck skipping and laughing and dashing in her wonderful, innocent world. "Good, good, great, you little thing!" he would call to her, and when he had framed and captured just what he was after, that perfect moment where light and shadow and color and movement and face and feel were all combined to his liking, he rose and ran for her and swept an arm around her in congratulation.

I tell you this story of a picture's creation because most recently the name of Gordon Parks has been associated with the searingly realistic photographs he has taken of poverty in the black ghetto and the plight of his people. Photographs don't always have to be a record of what is—direct and untarnished by some of the imaginative things a lens and film can do when in the right hands and directed by the right eye and heart. Photographs can be created images— a mood, a flash, a flavor—and for decades Gordon Parks has been a pioneer and innovator in this sort of creative photography, first in the world of fashion, then with his poetic interpretations of literature, of places, of times.

In his autobiography, A Choice of Weapons, Gordon Parks told the story of the truly great decision of his life: to wage his own personal battle against the world and for it, by using photography and words and music in place of fists and guns and blood. It would have been easy for him to take the other course. He had good reason for it—a Kansas childhood filled with poverty, violence, and discrimination; hunger and bitterness which at one point drew him almost to the point of robbery with a switchblade knife; humiliation; and fights growing out of that humiliation that would have left a lesser athlete and man dead in the gutter.

But there was always something inside this man—which he forced out of himself, forced to flower and bear fruit—and that was the poet's sense—his eye, his ear, his soul. A goodly quantity of those fruits is contained in this volume.

Here we have a series of poetic images, flashes of photographic insights mingled with word poems—some connected, some not. The book begins with a haunting image of peace. In his first picture Gordon Parks has allowed the light spraying through his camera lens to shower upon a dove wrapped in darkness with only a speck of background to highlight the mystery of its setting.

The whiteness of the bird is broken up, mottled with dark crystalline feather tones. The rim of its back is shaded with blue light that is repeated above in a blob of blue that seems to be on winged flight to the one tiny patch of reality at the top of the picture, a hint of leaf and sky. It is a dove of memory—as the accompanying poem will tell you—seen long ago "in an inkling of bougain-villaea," silent now, but still capable of song to him who might listen.

The poems, both words and pictures, continue, gentle mostly, many idealistic in theme and highly romantic. They are of a mother pregnant, a boy suddenly learning who he is, a longing for a lost moment of innocence, the humble blessings of family and shelter, a good life summed up by the possessions on a desk, the passion of old age. Gordon Parks sings about love, a lost love, a love had, a love explained, a love feared. A tiger strides across two pages, silhouetted against a stalky shimmer of rippled blue, again a shadow, a mystery. Winged nun hats almost take flight, birds fill a fiery sunset over a city, the sun bursts like a star against the glass lens, the Uirapurú cries its heart-tearing night song, weaving melodic magic lure of love. Words and pictures meld, free themselves from one another, meld again. Soon it becomes clear that it is the image that counts, not whether that image is displayed in photographs or words. Read and look at this book carefully and I think you will agree that Gordon Parks' choice of weapons was an important choice for you and me.

PHILIP B. KUNHARDT, JR.

THE DOVE

It was here
In an inkling of bougainvillaea
Then we met beneath its singing
Wandered in its meaning
Curious,
Hopeful and foreglimpsing
Knowing little of
                    (and how could we)
The systems of things
Due for violent turning.
In the dusk of that evening
We parted
To the crimson voice of war.
Now
Time, nibbling through pain
And Death
Has freed me. If only
You exist somewhere
Perhaps
Again we might hear its singing.

# THE ROAD

I have traveled this road so long that
Perhaps I have helped to shape its course.
Often now when I return upon it
Torn and limp from the day's labor
The trees, tall and aware, lean over
Whispering that home is just ahead.
I go on, to the rising noise of children
And the barking of a hound or two,
Until I see a lifetime's worth
For which that day was spent—
                              a lamp
Glowing warm through a curtained window.

Like a chilling waterfall
splashing,
unannounced,
upon the heat of
an Indian's naked back,
the Uirapurú,
as it dips and soars,
wings trembling, feathers
aflutter,
screams its heart-tearing
night song over a
suddenly silent jungle.
And all things hopping,
walking,
crawling,
flying,
slithering in the
mossy blackness
—the toad, the tiger,
the leopard, the spider,
the flamingo, wild heron,
the glowworm,
the toucan, the python—
fix their eyes on
the worshiping Indian
who,
caught in the magic of
melodic lure,
goes in crazed search of
the sweet agonizing cry—
the cry of Uirapurú,
their evasive king of love.

# AN EVENING TALE

Liquid night,
Soured by scornful dawn,
                    sent
Thoughtbuds into reeling.
Sober-hunger,
Scorched with tiredless hurt,
                    pushed
Soul to inner cursing.
Truthless voice,
Spurned by morning birdsong,
                    set
Ears to painful listening.
Faithless bed,
Damned by oath undone,
                    shot
His heart to shallow grieving.

## TO ALAIN

There's me!
Shining in the water-sun!
There's me!
With all the fishes, weeds and things!
Me moves when I move!
Me laughs when I laugh! And
There's a crooked sky and a
White bird flying through a turtle's shell!
But tell me
Where goes day each night? And
Where goes night all day?
How far is the sky up?
How deep is the earth down? And
What puffs up clouds and wets the rain?
Who pulls the river and blows the wind?
I can fly my kite and catch butterflies,
I can even climb a tree! But tell me
Why can't I outrun my shadow?

# FALSE SPRING

Months later, his skiff tied in, he set his
Quivering foot upon the mossbank. It was spring
And she was there. The chimney smoke told him so.
He had come to ask what he had waited so long to ask.
He sent his thoughts flying back like wild geese
Across the fjord. His cabin—no longer the single
Silence of it in cold womanless winter. The table
Hewn for two would now be set for more than one.
The bed for love would know more than just the longing.
He lit his pipe and let his eye follow a mountain bird.
                              No use to hurry.
She was there. The chimney smoke told him so.
Through the dew flowers he walked slow, stopping now,
Thinking to the odor of dogwood and new spruce, to
The woman smell mixed of love sweat, the cry of child
Some future night. He knocked gently upon the door.
                              She was there,
Bellyround in rocking chair knitting things for child
To wear. But now a stranger fired the hearth.
He didn't tarry long—five minutes at the most.
But outside the air had chilled. The sun had gone.
Ice was on the dew flowers and mountain birds had
                              flown to roost.
He pushed off without looking back.
Behind him only the wrinkled fjord. He must hurry.
It could ice over before he reached the other shore.

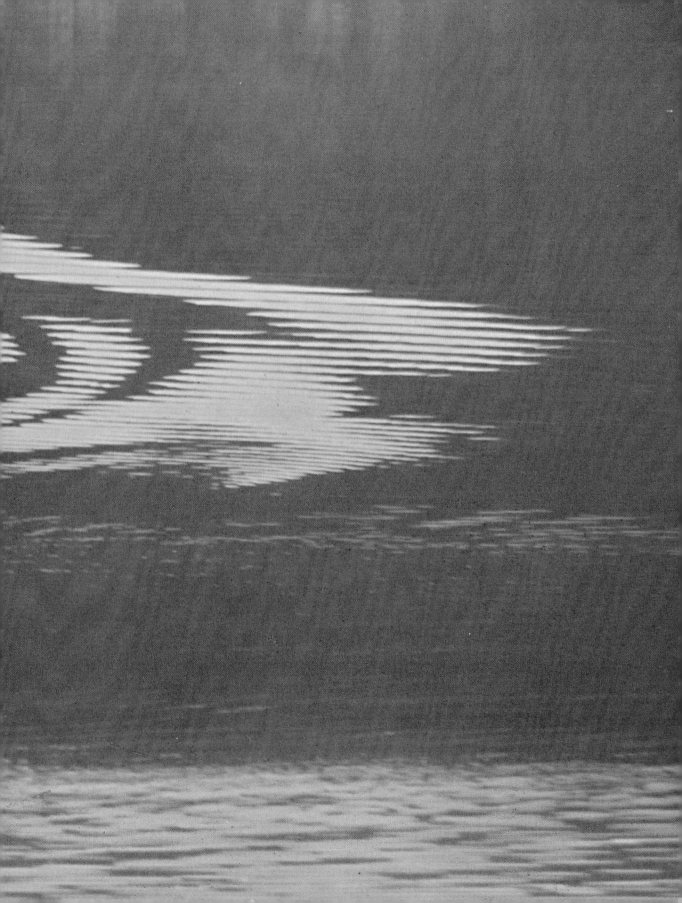

GRAVE DIGGER

What are you digging there young man?
A body hole for death old man.
Who do you dig it for young man?
For me old man for me. None other.
But why for one so young as you?
I'm looking ahead old man, for me.
But there's lots of time. Why rush
                              young fellow?
So that I, like you, might idle
                              near the end
To watch some young fellow digging.

With beauty gone,
The perimeter narrowing,
She strained against the inevitable.
She was forced along.
                              The energy
Consumed in the struggle
Hastened the collapse.
S'effondrer sans dignité.
S'effondrer sans honneur.

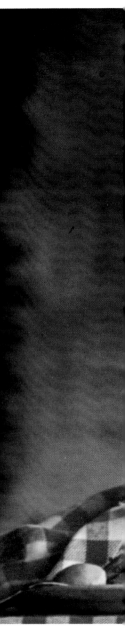

# THROUGH A TRAIN WINDOW

Hunger-eyed and sallow-cheeked
The child stared in at me, and
I stared back, full-bellied,
A vintage wine beside my plate.
No despair showed on her face,
None at least that I could see.
Just a trace of disbelief
That I ate there instead of she.

HOPE

Zelda likes waiting for things to happen
The night that never comes,
                                        death

For her lover's wife,
A bridge to collapse,
The voice that fails to call,
The seeds that never flower.
She awaits the soft white cloud
                        to step upon,
The strike of the blade into her breast,
The touch of a gentle hand upon her cheek.
For these and many other things she
                        waits
                                waits and
                                        waits.
Neglecting her desires, her power to attract.
These things, of course, may never happen. Yet
                        she knows.
The ridiculous thing, the important thing
                        is that

Zelda likes the waiting.

# LONELINESS

I was wed to it at birth
And I've made the best of it
I can't trust it
                    but I confide in it,
Without veiling the worst deed
                    or thought.
Recently in the cold sordid hours
It has become the only thing
That I can truly reason with.

## KANSAS LAND

I would miss this Kansas land that I was leaving.
Wide prairie filled of green and cornstalk;
                                   the flowering apple
Tall elms and oaks bordering streams that gurgle,
Rivers rolling quiet in long summers of sleepy days
For fishing, for swimming, for catching crawdad beneath
                                   the rock.
Cloud tufts billowing across the round blue sky.
Butterflies to chase through grass high as the chin.
Junebugs, swallowtails, red robin and bobolink,
Nights filled of soft laughter, fireflies and restless stars,
The winding sound of crickets rubbing dampness from their wings.
Silver September rain, orange-red-brown Octobers and
                             white Decembers with hungry
Smells of hams and pork butts curing in the smokehouse.
Yes, all this I would miss—along with the fear, hatred
                               and violence
We blacks had suffered upon this beautiful land.

# THE SEDUCTION

Marbled waves, restless, searching
Burst into the virgin cove.
She cupped salt tears from the spray
To cool the nightbed heat,
                          borrowed
The shadows of blue green brine to
Color the cruel sweet dark.
                          One minute,
Added to each hour winding down,
Prolonged the hunger-swollen tide.
She was blind to the liquid rose
Under whose look-through petals
                          she chose to hide.
They were stone heavy and
She has drowned beneath their weight.

## IS LOVE

Stiff from mystic sleep, psychedelic night
They stand there young woman young man
                                    warming
In hip morning sunlight,
Gone parts of some square mamma's dream
                        some big daddy's pride.
Enemy of napalm Washington and conformity,
Of flagwaving and honordraping
Of Brooks Brothers and cautious love.
Friend of indifference, protest and
                                    calamity,
Of flowers, of hair and unsocial things.
                        "Child,
Is this the way to run a young life?"
                        "You bet it is
Love is love is love is love
                        is love."

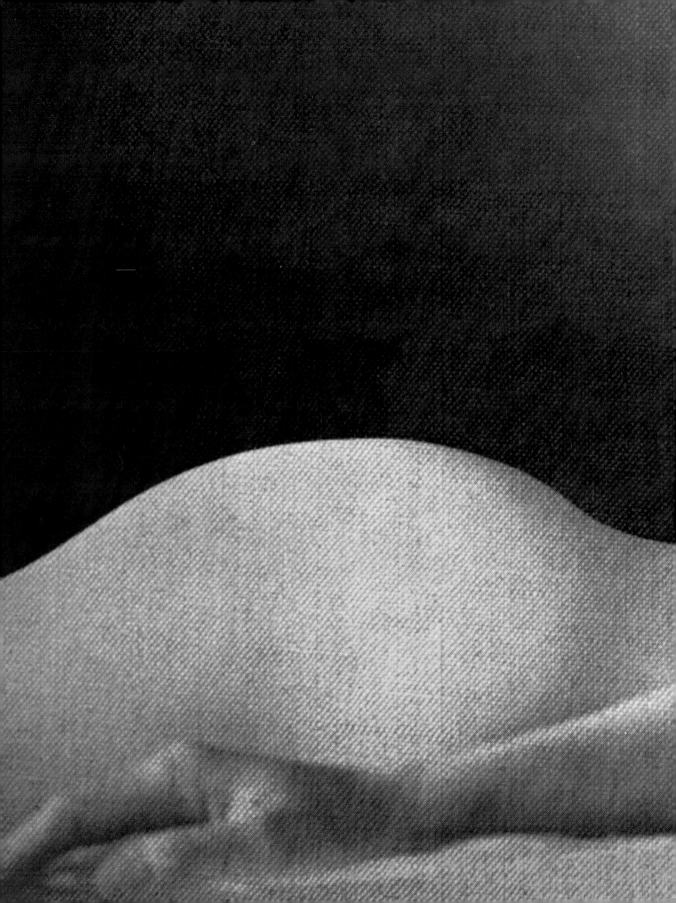

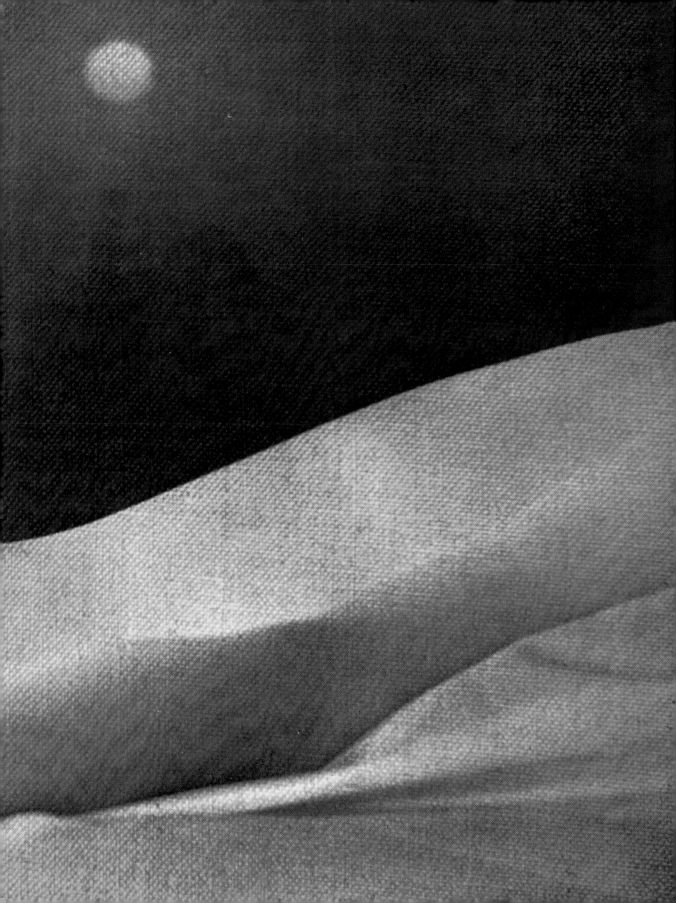

CHILD COMING

You are child-seed swelling now,
Stirring in the mother warmth.
Between some frantic sunup
                    or panicky moondown,
You will bolt the womb to
A nippled, milk-full world.
Your length will be measured,
                    not by infant inches,
But by seasons—
                    when spring is in your tears
When summer is in your cheeks
                    when autumn is in your voice
When winter is in your walk.
Your weight will be taken,
                    not in common pounds,
But in heartbreak points of coming time
                    when the moon is black
And stars melt in flames of brother-terror.
                                        But
You are only child-seed swelling now.
                              Strength
Awaits you in the expectant breast.

# MIDDLE AGE

These things, these people are the truth of me.
Unhurriedly, they gathered to share this desk.
The gold wedding clock there no longer ticks:
The silver shoe belonged to the boy we lost to war.
The ancient pen, wet still from mortgage pay,
Was Grandfather's then Father's—before it was mine.
My wife, smiling, but ill, our grandson on her knee,
Nursed and worried this house into a home.
Each morning I come to meet myself here, to feel
The everlastingness of what awaits. And
In the quiet of these earliest moments
I savor the immortal blossoming of man's
                                        eternal tree.

## OLD AGE

Snow covers the autumn leaf.
Time has granted me full cycle. I know
The wintry anguish of hunger, sickness—
                              family loss.
And more than once, man's ignobleness scraped
                              my heart, but
I don't cut easily to raw edges of things now.
I look back, without sadness, without nostalgia.
The full passion of living struck the balance.
This season, eternal, inevitable, signals
The coming of yet another. The end is not the end,
                              but
The whole purpose of the beginning. So,
These leaves mix with earth to nourish others.
                         And when snow is gone
They become the shade of another spring.

# FLIGHT OVER AFRICA

On through the mysterious African night we roar
pushing time, intercepting hours yet unlived,
while down through the Nubian desert heat the moon
shimmers on the Nile. And stars move with
us over Khartoum, lying small and jeweled in the
immeasurable blackness. So many empty spaces for
bush to grow and sands to roll. The world tilts and
we streak toward morning and Kenya. Dawn. A big red
ball of sun creeps up from the horizon and starts
spiking unmerciful heat into a sandstorm.
Pity those caught there in the evil *haboob*'s fierce beauty.
Miles below, where the endless brown river snakes
out from the desert, the riders stop their camels—and
there is good reason to stop. They kneel with their animals, and
the mountain of black swirls over their caravan. Speak to God for
them! Next, the mounts of Kenya and Kilimanjaro envy one
another's majesty. On southward: Kenya's wilderness, strung out in
all faraway directions, pillaged and evangelized for mortal stakes.
Tribes, rites, customs streaming through backward time; things fear-
some to man, leopard, lion and cobra alike. Beneath a cloud break, a
glint of sun summons our eyes, and there speaking the future is
Nairobi. We scream over, jarring hostile animal ears. Rhodesia
lies ahead. "Africa! Black Africa! She has chosen!" This proud
cry remembered as our quake scatters a herd of giraffe into grace-
ful loping. Hippo, bubbling in the slow-moving Zambezi, dive from
our noise. A pair of lions, used to the age of motors, drowsy and
more dangerous than they appear, crouch in the shade of a monkey
tree. We start down and Livingstone's Africa opens beneath us like
a giant flower. Then the awesome falls of Victoria, the melting
mountain, emptying unsparingly into its valley of constant rain.
Sundown and a single star, huge, hypnotic, brilliant, unbelievable,
hangs moon-bright over the River Zambezi, glittering the black
water. Only experience knows the truth of such beauty. Only our
memory holds it as we touch down in the coming dark.

IF AS YOU SAY

Before I took my mother's blood and breath
            I loved you.
When you broke the silence of your first hour,
                        crying
Through oval-slit eyes under some foreign sky,
I had already begun to guard your days.
            Each moonfall after,
I tossed a lotus petal into my river of dreams
Until an endless bouquet smothered the oceans
                                    that parted us.
Through winter-locked and hungered days,
                                    in
The mindshaped trials of doubt-filled years,
                        over
Hourless and mistaken roads I searched for you.
If as you say, during pillow-talk, you do not know me,
            It is because I am you.
I have been you for a thousand years.
            Our love is older than the air.

# DISCOVERY OF BRAZIL

The cross!
The cross!
The cross!
The blessed cross!
    in with the thankful,
            chanting Portuguese
from a punishing sea,
raised in host of
       first mass,
under the eye of Indian
          and beast alike.
Chants the priest,
*Kyrie eleison!*
Echoes the Indian,
(bless them spirit
    of our great sky)
*Christe eleison!*
(bless them O spirit
    of our fearful jungle)
*Kyrie eleison!*
(bless them spirit
    of striped leopard)
*Kyrie eleison!*
(bless them O spirit
    of all running waters)
The true cross!
Chalice, incense, tinkling bells
    upon the land
       of
    Cruziero do Sul.

NIGHT FEAR

The world smiled in on them
And, through pristine skies,
Lit the mornings of their youth.
Then, their faces lifted to the light,
A sparrow-sliced and wondrous light
That flashed upon spring boughs. And the hours
Breathed of rosebud and new grass.
What lay ahead was time-silenced, unpledged.
And dreams were filled with balloons and carousels.

The ancient walls, peopled and shrewd,
Stored the mingled laughter, knowing
From time over, a future need of it.
Their youth, so given to the instant's pleasure,
Held few memories with which to stay itself.
Each day was better than each yesterday, and
Every nightfall was more star-etched, more
Moon-radiant than any others. Eternally,
It seemed, the world would smile.

It was long after their vows were taken.
He tended a November fire. She,
Sewing at the window, saw the bird flock,
Wind-driven, dipping, darkening the roseate sky.
"They blacken the day like clouds," she said.
But when the shadowing flight passed on
Dark remained, ruffled like chimney smoke over
Winter afternoon. With such blowing out of doors
She stirred uneasily, her eyes questioning the
Clock on the blistered wall. "Ivan, it is only two,
Yet night has come." Gruffly, without once thinking,
He answered, "Should I adjust the time, Amy—or
Perhaps the light?" Then he turned back to the fire
And his thoughts.

Weighted now with woman hurt she took the stairs
To their sunless room. And there for
A memoried and startled moment, she saw
Their portraits, painted an afternoon ago.
Side by side, the portraits stared at her.
And suddenly she knew his thoughts. Yes she knew.
His rosebud had been fresh that day, but
Withered now, it drooped from his lapel. Strange—
She remembered the grass where she stood as green.
Now it looked trampled and parched. "Dear Ivan,"
She sighed, and lay upon their bed.

Walking that evening, both equally gray, both
Quiet as the river traveling the cobbled bank,
They heard, they thought, a discordant wail.
He was first to glance back—he shivered.
"What is it?" she asked, drawing close.
"An old lady stands beside a dying tree."
The wail again, and this time she looked.
"Why lie, Ivan? It is an old man."
They walked on, silent, a chill at their backs.

She watched him from the stairway that night.
And he saw her reflected in a silver urn,
Saw her go through the door then pull back,
Fright upon her face. And he went up to her.

Asking, with labored breath, "What bothers you?
Speak, Amy! Of what are you so deathly afraid?"
Tightly, she held his hand, weeping now for him.
And he knew that she knew his fear.
Yet, cowardly, he started to ask again. Instead—
"Amy." His arms dropped in truth. "Yes, I took my

Portrait away. He was stupid, the painter on the quai.
The old idiot couldn't see. Such lies he framed in gold
Upon our dresser. I tell you he was blind."
Stiff in agony, she turned away to leave him there
Trembling. And she entered the room alone,
Whispering as she went, "One face is yours,
The other mine. Fairest of flowers fade in time.
One face is yours, the other mine."

It was late when he came in. She was waiting.
He lay beside her, wordless; still she waited.
At last he spoke. "I am beside you, Amy. Do you hear?
I am beside you. Being together is enough."
With no pretense at sleep, she drew close.
"Each new morning nudges us forward," she murmured.
"From tree to tree, from shadow to shadow," he agreed.
"We are not alone, Ivan. Hear the voices within our walls?"

And they lay close, listening, as young laughter
Drowned out wind of the aged night. And all
The sky smiled in upon them, cloudless, deep
                                        And star-silent.

# BLACK GLADIATOR

Into the dark arena I came
Searching for what you always
Kept from me. And you
Watched from the shadows,
                              laughing
Through the cold blackness,
Your sword hard upon my need.
And darkness piled upon darkness
Until the very blackness of it
                      made light.
Light that caught you in my rebellious glare.
Perhaps you might have escaped
Were it not for your fear.

## TARDE AZUL  (Blue Dusk)

I lie here reed-thin, needled with lament
Under a chalk moon with bored flamingos watching.
                              Here
Where grief torments memory of things past
                                        things dead
Things far beyond some miraculous awakening.
And between tireless stars and white-robed river
Reality comes on wings of things we knew
                              and loved together,
In some full-grown night of a withered yesterday.
                              Here,
This past and I lie alone on this weed bed
Sharing traitorous guilt with the white-winged watchers
Above me; the stubborn, innocent waterflow beside me.
And all that might have happened in some evening dusk
Is as claimless as silence of the half-grown moon.
No sleep for the anguished night. No waking
                              here
                    In the threatening dawn.

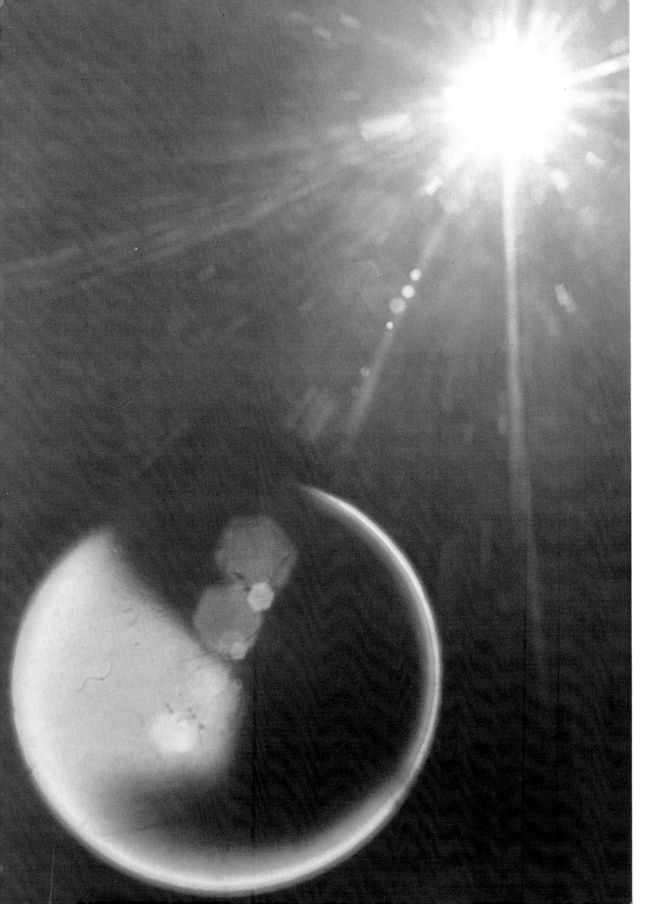